A GIFT FOR:

_____

FROM:

_____

FRESH-CUT
Flowers
FOR
MOTHER

J COUNTRYMAN®

www.jcountryman.com
A division of Thomas Nelson, Inc.
www.thomasnelson.com

Hundreds of dewdrops to greet the dawn,
Hundreds of bees in the purple clover,
Hundreds of butterflies on the lawn,
But only one mother the wide world over.

GEORGE COOPER

Lessons learned at mother's knee last through life.

LAURA INGALLS WILDER

Trust in the LORD with all your heart, and lean not on your own understanding; in all your ways acknowledge Him, and He shall direct your paths.

PROVERBS 3:5-6

The work of righteousness will be peace,
and the effect of righteousness,
quietness and assurance forever.

ISAIAH 32:17

A life touched by God
always ends in
touching others.

ERWIN MCMANUS

The eternal God is your refuge,
and underneath are
the everlasting arms.

DEUTERONOMY 33:27

No matter what our
journeys lead us
through, we always
end up in God.

LESLIE WILLIAMS

The mother is and must be,
whether she knows it or not, the
greatest, strongest, and most
lasting teacher her children have.

HANNAH WHITALL SMITH

Charm is deceitful and beauty is passing,
but a woman who fears the LORD,
she shall be praised.

PROVERBS 31:30

Love is, above all,

the gift of oneself.

JEAN ANOUILH

God gives us friends—

and that means much;

but far above all others,

the greatest of His gifts

to earth was when He

thought of mothers.

ANONYMOUS

It is a gift that lasts
through all our days.

One mother achieves more
than a hundred teachers.

YIDDISH PROVERB

Make our sons in their prime
like sturdy oak trees,
our daughters as shapely and
bright as fields of wildflowers.

PSALM 144:12
THE MESSAGE

*How comforting to think of the love
that always fills a mother's heart
and spills over into the home.*

Love begins at home.

MOTHER TERESA

Every good gift
and every perfect
gift is from above,
and comes down
from the Father of
lights.

JAMES 1:17

All of life is a gift, and God
has given it for joy.

TERRY LINDVALL

Who ran to help me when I fell,

And would some pretty story tell,

Or kiss the place to make it well?

My Mother.

ANNE TAYLOR

Her children rise up
and call her blessed.

PROVERBS 31:28

Who can ever measure
the benefit of a
mother's inspiration?

CHARLES R. SWINDOLL

*I owe heaven an
unpayable debt for giving
me a God-fearing mother.*

There is no friendship, no love, like
that of the parent for the child.

HENRY WARD BEECHER

More than my mother,
you are my friend.
That makes me glad!

God is greater than our heart,
and knows all things.

1 JOHN 3:20

God is always far
more willing to give
us good things
than we are
anxious to have them.

CATHERINE
MARSHALL

23

Mother's apron gave you assurance. Rushing in from school or play, even if you didn't see or hear her, you felt better just finding that apron hanging behind the kitchen door or dangling across a chair. Her apron, smelling of cookies and starch and Mother. It comforted you. It made you feel secure. It was part of her—like her laugh or her eyes.

MARJORIE HOLMES

Blessed are the
people who know
the joyful sound!

PSALM 89:15

Joy is the normal result of a
heart burning with love.

MOTHER TERESA

The LORD is good to all,
and His tender mercies are
over all His works.

PSALM 145:9

God's fingers can touch

nothing but to mould it

into loveliness.

GEORGE MACDONALD

Delight yourself
also in the LORD,
and He shall give
you the desires of
your heart.

PSALM 37:4

The heart that has no agenda
but God's is the heart at
leisure from itself.

ELISABETH ELLIOT

Nobody knows of the work it makes
To keep the home together,
Nobody knows of the steps it takes,
Nobody knows—but mother.

ANONYMOUS

29

You have to love your

children unselfishly.

That's hard.

But it's the only way.

BARBARA BUSH

Love suffers long and is kind; . . .
bears all things, believes all things,
hopes all things, endures all things.

1 CORINTHIANS 13:4

A mother is like a veil: she
hides the faults of her children.

YIDDISH PROVERB

Let us love one another,
for love is of God.

1 JOHN 4:7

I know what I'm doing. I have it all planned out—plans to take care of you, not abandon you, plans to give you the future you hope for.

JEREMIAH 29:11, THE MESSAGE

God is highly confident
of His own plans.

KATHY TROCCOLI

It is God who arms me with strength, and makes my way perfect.

PSALM 18:32

If any of you lacks
wisdom, let him ask
of God, who gives to
all liberally and without
reproach, and it will
be given to him.

JAMES 1:5

A mother understands
what a child does not say.

ANONYMOUS

Even now you seem
to read my thoughts
and feel what my
heart feels, but cannot say.

The LORD is good; His mercy is everlasting, and His truth endures to all generations.

PSALM 100:5

Teach us to escape the worries of this world, to live and rest in You.

HARRIET CROSBY

Dear child, if you become wise,
I'll be one happy parent.
My heart will dance and sing
to the tuneful truth you'll speak.

PROVERBS 23:13, THE MESSAGE

We are wise by
other people's
experience.

SAMUEL
RICHARDSON

Knowledge from books;

wisdom from life.

JEWISH PROVERB

We watch and want to be
the good that we see.

Now thank we all our God,

With hearts, and hands and voices,

Who wondrous things has done,

In whom His world rejoices;

Who from our mother's arms

Has blessed us on our way

With countless gifts of love,

And still is ours today.

MARTIN RINKART

41

The measure
of love is
compassion;
the measure
of compassion
is kindness.

ANONYMOUS

I'm so touched by your
compassion, which reaches far
beyond our family to so many
who need a touch of kindness.

Nothing means as
much as my dear
mother's tender touch.

Mothers must model
the tenderness we
need. Our world can't
find it anywhere else.

CHARLES R. SWINDOLL

43

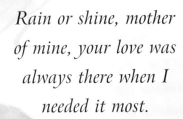

*Rain or shine, mother
of mine, your love was
always there when I
needed it most.*

A noble heart is a

changeless heart.

ANONYMOUS

He has made everything
beautiful in its time.

ECCLESIASTES 3:11

The Lord's goodness is the
source of all our joy.

C. H. SPURGEON

No woman can be strong,

gentle, pure, and good without

the world being better for it,

without somebody being

helped and comforted

by the very existence

of that goodness.

PHILLIPS BROOKS

Blessed are the pure in heart,
for they shall see God.

MATTHEW 5:8

He will love you and bless
you and multiply you.

DEUTERONOMY 7:13

You cannot
always *have*
happiness,
but you can
always give
happiness.

ANONYMOUS

That habit of giving only
enhances the desire to give.

WALT WHITMAN

Your generous heart gives out
to others and makes them
want to give back to you.

They're only truly great
who are truly good.

GEORGE CHAPMAN

I think you're great,
because you're a truly
good mom!

The supreme
happiness of life is
the conviction that
we are loved; loved
for ourselves—
rather, loved in
spite of ourselves.

VICTOR HUGO

He will rejoice over you
with gladness, He will
quiet you with His love.

ZEPHANIAH 3:17

In the final analysis it is
not what you do for your
children but what you
have taught them to do
for themselves that will
make them successful
human beings.

ANN LANDERS

He who has begun a good
work in you will complete it
until the day of Jesus Christ.

PHILIPPIANS 1:6

*I have no doubt God chuckled
to think of your surprising
personality, and sighed with
contentment to know what a
wonderful mother you'd be.*

When God thought of
Mother, He must have
laughed with satisfaction—
so rich, so deep, so full of
power and beauty was the
conception.

HENRY WARD BEECHER

May the LORD give you
increase more and more,
You and your children.
May you be blessed
by the LORD,
Who made heaven
and earth.

PSALM 115:14-15

Thank you for teaching me that God is love, that His love is never-ending.

I remember my mother, my father and the rest of us praying together each evening. It is God's greatest gift to the family.

MOTHER TERESA

Mama was like a flowing
river, blessing the banks
of life around her.

MARGARET JENSEN

Oh, God, for others let me be,
at least half the blessing
my dear Mother has been to me.

You filled my life
with the wealth of
wisdom that comes
from loving God.

No one is poor who
had a godly mother.

ABRAHAM LINCOLN

God's love did not begin at Calvary.
Before the world was baptized with the
first light, before the first blades of
tender grass peeped out, God was love.

BILLY GRAHAM

I have loved you with
an everlasting love.

JEREMIAH 31:3

She opens
her mouth
with wisdom
and on her
tongue is the law
of kindness.

PROVERBS 31:26

A little rain can straighten a flower stem.
A little love can change a life.

MAX LUCADO

Joy is knowing your
mom loves you,
even (especially)
when you don't
deserve to be loved.

Blessed are

the joy-makers.

NATHANIEL
PARKER WILLIS

A gracious woman retains honor.

PROVERBS 11:16

Your kindness to me
let me see
how to be kind to others.

We are made
kind by
being kind.

ERIC HOFFER

Give your cares to Him who
cares for the flowers of the field.
Rest assured He will also
care for you.

C. H. SPURGEON

My help
comes from
the LORD, who
made heaven
and earth.

PSALM 121:1

Let the

hearts of

those rejoice

who seek the

LORD.

PSALM 105:3

Finding joy means first of all
finding Jesus.

JILL BRISCOE

[She] who sows bountifully
will also reap bountifully.

2 CORINTHIANS 9:6

There is no
happiness in
having or in
getting, but
only in giving.

HENRY
DRUMMOND

68

Mercy is
the deepest
gesture of
kindness.

MAX
LUCADO

There is gold and a multitude of
rubies, but the lips of knowledge
are a precious jewel.

PROVERBS 20:15

Life is the first gift,

love the second,

and understanding

the third.

MARGE PIERCY

No one has given more to my
life than you, Mother.

Mother's love grows by giving.

CHARLES LAMB

Everything
I learned
about love,
I learned
from my
mother.

MARITA
GOLDEN

I learned things like
a hug can let you
know you're special.

You made our home a sanctuary—a haven from the hectic, harried, world outside.

The woman
is the heart
of the home.

MOTHER TERESA

There is no greater place
of ministry, position,
or power than that
of a mother.

PHIL WHISENHUNT

God could
use a few
more mothers,
like mine.

The wise woman builds her house.

PROVERBS 14:1

The older I get, the more
I marvel at the work and
determination you poured into
making our house a home, not only
a beautiful home but a godly home.

There is no more
influential or
powerful role
on earth than
a mother's.

CHARLES R.
SWINDOLL

You have been one of the most
positive and significant influences
in my life. Thank you for being a
wonderful role model.

I honor you mother. Not just for giving me life, but for making my life a gift.

Honor your father and mother, even as you honor God, for all three were partners in your creation.

JEWISH PROVERB

Whatever things you ask in prayer,

believing, you will receive.

MATTHEW 21:22

*Praying unlocks the doors of heaven
and releases the power of God.*

BILLY GRAHAM

To love someone more
dearly every day,
To help a wandering child
to find his way,
To ponder o'er a noble
thought and pray,
And smile when evening
falls—this is my task.

MAUDE LOUISE RAY

81

I always seek the good that is in people and leave the bad to Him who made mankind and knows how to round off the corners.

GOETHE'S MOTHER

How glad we can
be that God does
indeed let us leave
the rounding
off to Him.

She who gives all,
though but little,
gives much.

QUARLES

*Even when we didn't have much,
you taught us to give generously.
You were teaching us how to open
the door of God's rich blessings not
only for our lives but for others.*

Mom, you are truly
one of God's greatest
gifts to me.

I thank God for
my mother as for
no other gift of
His bestowing.

WILLARD

How precious also
are Your thoughts
to me, O God!
How great is the
sum of them!

PSALM 139:17

Mothers
have big
aprons—to
cover the
faults of their
children.

JEWISH
PROVERB

Every kid needs a mother's
forgiving heart to hide behind.

He cares for you.

1 PETER 5:7

God wants only the best for us.
He likes to treat each one of us
as if we were an only child.

INGRID TROBISCH

I remember my mother's prayers . . . and they have clung to me all my life.

I will always count on your prayers, Mom.

If you were blessed with a good mother, you will reap the benefits all of your days.

CHARLES R. SWINDOLL

Mom, the legacy of your love
goes on and on and on.